# COCONUT

by Guleraana Mir

## ‖SAMUEL FRENCH‖

**samuelfrench.co.uk**

# THINKING ABOUT PERFORMING A SHOW?

**There are thousands of plays and musicals available to perform from Samuel French right now, and applying for a licence is easier and more affordable than you might think**

---

From classic plays to brand new musicals, from monologues to epic dramas, there are shows for everyone.

Plays and musicals are protected by copyright law so if you want to perform them, the first thing you'll need is a licence. This simple process helps support the playwright by ensuring they get paid for their work, and means that you'll have the documents you need to stage the show in public.

Not all our shows are available to perform all the time, so it's important to check and apply for a licence before you start rehearsals or commit to doing the show.

## LEARN MORE & FIND THOUSANDS OF SHOWS

Browse our full range of plays and musicals and find out more about how to license a show

**www.samuelfrench.co.uk/perform**

Talk to the friendly experts in our Licensing team for advice on choosing a show, and help with licensing

**plays@samuelfrench.co.uk   020 7387 9373**

# *Acting* Editions
## BORN TO PERFORM

### Playscripts designed from the ground up to work the way you do in rehearsal, performance and study

---

*Larger*, clearer text for easier reading

*Wider* margins for notes

*Performance features* such as character and props lists, sound and lighting cues, and more

---

## + CHOOSE A SIZE AND STYLE TO SUIT YOU

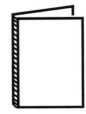

**STANDARD EDITION**

Our regular paperback book at our regular size

**SPIRAL-BOUND EDITION**

The same size as the Standard Edition, but with a sturdy, easy-to-fold, easy-to-hold spiral-bound spine

**LARGE EDITION**

A4 size and spiral bound, with larger text and a blank page for notes opposite every page of text. Perfect for technical and directing use

LEARN MORE    samuelfrench.co.uk/actingeditions

**OVALHOUSE**

"a founding father of today's fringe theatre" *Guardian*

For the past 50 years Ovalhouse has been a home to experimental, radical and overlooked artists seeking to make theatre and performance that speaks to a world beyond the mainstream.
A hotbed of artistic activism in the five decades since we began, Ovalhouse has seen the social and artistic ideals it has aspired to become widely accepted as the model for a better society. We have sheltered social and political movements staffed by the stage and screen stars of the future, and pursued an unerring agenda for positive artistic, political and social change. Ovalhouse stands on a proud history and continues to be a vital home for boundary-pushing art and artists with an eye on the future.

Ovalhouse has been known for its support for artists - professional and young people – for over 50 years – commissioning new work that responds to today's social and political issues, and work that reflects the cultural diversity of its local community.

ovalhouse.com | @ovalhouse

### Ovalhouse Staff

Director: Deborah Bestwick
Executive Producer: Stella Kanu
General Manager: Gary Johnson
Head of Theatre & Artist Development: Owen Calvert-Lyons
Head of Learning & Participation: Mahri Reilly
Technical Manager: Sam Evans

Learning & Participation Manager: Titilola Dawudu
Producing Coordinator: Will Bourdillon
Demonstrate Projects Manager: Elena Molinaro
Building Projects Manager: Annika Brown
Finance Administrator: Kwame T B Antwi
Trusts & Foundations Manager: John Peterson
Development Director – Capital Campaign: Katie Milton
Operations Manager: Alex Clarke
Duty Managers: Lily Batikyan, Stephanie Prior, James York

Ovalhouse | 52-54 Kennington Oval | London | SE11 5SW
Tel: 020 7582 0080 | Box Office: 020 7582 7680 | info@ovalhouse.com

Supported using public funding by
**ARTS COUNCIL ENGLAND**
LOTTERY FUNDED

# THE THELMAS

The Thelmas are dedicated to the development and promotion of female writers. They passionately support new writing from unheard voices and actively promote BAMER stories. They aim to create and support work that resists the temptation to problematise being female, and instead disrupts traditional stereotypes. The Thelmas are:

## GULERAANA MIR – Writer

Guleraana is a playwright and applied theatre practitioner. She is passionate about creating diverse stories that are rooted in our modern society and committed to using her voice to explore what makes us human; all the things that we do to, and for each other.

Her first full-length play, *Shooting Star,* was longlisted by BBC's SCRIPTROOM 8. She was one of the first writers to work with Almeida Theatre Projects schools residency and part of the Tamasha Theatre playwriting group 2016/2017. She regularly writes for community and youth groups and has recently worked with AGE UK Westminster and Rightful Place Theatre, a theatre company made up of Mulberry School staff and alumni. Her professional work has been supported by Theatre Delicatessen, Park Theatre and New Diorama Theatre. *Coconut* is her debut production.

## MADELAINE MOORE – Direction and Dramaturgy

Madelaine is a freelance director, producer, applied theatre practitioner and founder of The Thelmas. She has worked extensively with diverse marginalised groups in the community, in custodial settings and, more recently, on professional productions.

Her most recent production, *The Awakening* (Jack Studio Theatre) earned multiple OFFIE and Broadway World nominations. Other credits include *If I Ran the Circus* (Discover Story Children's Centre), *W;T* and *Widows* (T-Junction Festival). She is also a visiting Director and Lecturer at St Mary's University, Twickenham, and the Royal Central School of Speech and Drama. *Coconut* will mark the first full-length play she has developed from scratch as dramaturg and director for The Thelmas.

*Coconut* premiered at Ovalhouse 11–28 April 2018 as a co-production between The Thelmas and Ovalhouse, followed by a National Tour with the following cast and creatives:

**RUMI** – Kuran Dohil
**SIMON** – Jimmy Riani-Carter
**RIZ/IRFAN** – Tibu Fortes

**MADELAINE MOORE** – Direction & Dramaturgy
**BASKA WESOLOWSKA** – Design
**JENNIFER ROSE** – Lighting Design
**LUCY MYERS** – Stage Management
**CO-PRODUCED BY THE THELMAS**

The production has been supported by Arts Council England, Park Theatre, New Diorama Theatre and In Good Company.

---

## TOUR DATES:

11–28 April  Ovalhouse, London
16 May  ARC Stockton Arts Centre, Stockton on Tees
19 May  Derby Theatre, Derby
24 May  Oldham Coliseum, Oldham
26 May  The Curve, Slough
18 June  Guildhall Arts Centre, Grantham
19 June  Brewhouse Arts Centre, Burton upon Trent
25 June  Old Fire Station, Oxford  (as part of Offbeat Festival)
27 June  Lincoln Drill Hall, Lincoln
28 June  Old Library, Mansfield
29 June  South Holland Centre, Spalding
30 June  Attenborough Arts Centre, Leicester

Supported using public funding by
**ARTS COUNCIL ENGLAND**
LOTTERY FUNDED

## AUTHOR'S NOTE

*Coconut,* started as a fifteen-minute monologue as part of Ladylogue!, an evening of one-woman shorts produced by The Thelmas. When artistic director Madelaine asked me what I wasn't writing about, I realised that I hadn't really explored my heritage in my playwriting at all. I decided my contribution to the project would be a character that was really honest about how confusing it is to be British born and brown – something that I've felt since I was a teenager. Cue Rumi and her desperate attempt to find a place where she belongs.

In developing the full-length version I have taken so many aspects of myself, and things that I have experienced, and given them to the characters. That said, it is definitely not an autobiography, or a blow-by-blow retelling of my marriage! *Coconut* is simply inspired by the truth of people like me, hours of research into conversion (or reversion), and the road to fundamentalism.

*Coconut* is the story of two people who aren't entirely comfortable in their own skin, or where they sit in society, trying to build a life together. One of them happens to be brown, and the other white. Some of their obstacles are pretty large. Religion, faith and cultural differences are major themes in the play, but so is the question – how far would you go to make the people you love happy? For Rumi the answer is pretty far, but as we find out the only thing that ever really works is being true to yourself, and ultimately that is the decision that both Rumi and Simon are forced to make.

The character of Riz represents Rumi's "inner voice". He is everything that she is feeling and unwilling to articulate out loud. We all have that voice that tells us what we should be doing, but it happens to be stronger and louder for those of us who identify with being cross-cultural. There is always the pressure to comply, and the fear that whatever you do, you will be judged, and in trying to please everyone you end up failing yourself.

Scenes between Rumi and Riz are described as being "in her world". There should be something ethereal about them – not entirely in the real world, but not so dream like that we're transported out of modern-day London.

*Coconut* was written to be accessible to all audiences, and should be staged in a somewhat naturalistic fashion that is easy to follow. It is a complicated story that needs to be told simply.

As part of the original production, Madelaine has compiled a wonderful soundtrack that best represents the meeting of two cultures, but we invite others to find a musicality that best suits them.

Please note that all performances in the original run at Ovalhouse (and most of the tour dates) included captioning using The Difference Engine, a discreet new tool for making events and performance accessible to partially sighted, deaf or hard of hearing audience members by delivering captioning or audio description direct to their mobile device. The Thelmas, and the author champion the notion that theatre is for all and ask that you make the effort to use this, or similar technology as part of any future productions, as we believe it is invaluable to growing new audiences.

## ON LANGUAGE

Translation to Urdu or Punjabi words are provided in bold next to the dialogue.
"/" Denotes an overlapping in dialogue
"—" Denotes an interruption
"..." Denotes an unspoken reaction

## DEDICATION/ACKNOWLEDGEMENTS

*Coconut* is what it is because so many people have been so generous with their time, ideas and support. My thanks go to: Sukh Ojla, who originated the role of Rumi and spent so long on this journey with us.

Karl Sedgwick, our first Simon, who helped us create a path for the character.

The current cast, obviously. Especially Tibu and Jimmy, who breathed life into their characters in a uniquely personal way. Fin Kennedy, who helped me reconnect with the play, its characters and why I was writing it in the first place.

The teams at Park Theatre, New Diorama, In Good Company and Ovalhouse, who believed in this story enough to take a chance by either putting it on their stage, or supporting with rehearsal space, feedback and answering of many questions.

Arts Council England.

Madelaine, producer and director extraordinaire. Thank you for constantly wanting to overturn the system, and believing that I am the right person to do it with you. For not only thinking that *Coconut* was worth investing your time in, but doing literally everything to get us to this stage. And of course, thank you for introducing me to the world of GIFs.

Thank you to my parents for not only allowing me to be a coconut, but then celebrating it when I turned it into a play.

And thank you Ben, for being you, and not Simon.

## CHARACTERS

RUMI – A British Pakistani woman, 25–35
SIMON – A British Caucasian man, 27–35
IRFAN (the imaam) – A British Asian man
RIZ – the voice inside Rumi's head, her "moral compass"
(IRFAN and RIZ can be played by the same actor)

## SETTING

London, modern day.

# ACT ONE

## Scene One

*We are in* **RUMI**'s *world. It might be her bedroom, or not, but it is a space where she is able to be honest and have a good, long word with herself. Lights rise on* **RUMI**, *a British Pakistani woman wearing an abaya and a headscarf, staring into the audience as if into a mirror.*

**RUMI**  As-salamu alaykum.

*It needs a little something, to be more formal, so she brings her palms together and nods.*

As-salamu alaykum.

*It's not right either, so she shakes it off. Taking a deep breath, she bows low with arms out, exhaling.*

As-salamu alaykum.

*She rises.* **RIZ** *speaks, as if from nowhere.*

**RIZ**  You kind of look like like Michael Jackson doing Jesus at the Brit Awards.

**RUMI**  Shit. I totally do.

*Beat.*

**RIZ**  Love your outfit, is it the new Sana Safinaz? Exquisite fabric.

**RUMI**  Desperate times call for desperate measures.

**RIZ**  Don't talk about yourself like that.

**RUMI**  Situation's getting dire.

**RIZ**  Nothing we can't handle in a sensible and strategic manner.

RUMI  Mum keeps shoving printouts of boys from shaadi.com under my door. She's desperate for me to get married.

RIZ  And the response is to put on an abaya and take up celibacy? / Don't know if I'm ready for that.

RUMI  / Quite the opposite. I'm going halal speed dating.

RIZ  In a bin bag?

RUMI  Choop oh. [**Oh be quiet**]

RIZ  Wearing that doesn't make you a good Muslim.

RUMI  Might make me look like one though.

RIZ  Just be yourself.

RUMI  Because that's worked out so well?

RIZ  And what are we going to do once we've bagged a prize brother?

RUMI  Just hide out. In plain sight.

RIZ  Your hobbies include mojitos and dancing. Do you even remember a single word of the Quran?

RUMI  Two coconuts drinking chai, watching Bollywood movies and doing shots of tequila at our three-day wedding. Not completely infeasible, is it?

RIZ  ...

RUMI  I didn't say the plan wasn't flawed, but I've got to do something. Can't keep disappointing everyone.

RIZ  Somewhere out there, there's a boy, nay a man who – who's just perfect.

RUMI  What's he look like?

RIZ  A delightful mix of Raza Jaffrey, Riz Ahmed and Zayn Malik.

RUMI  ...

RIZ  Okay, not Zayn Malik. Just Raza and Riz.

RUMI  Riza.

RIZ  Riza.

RUMI  And what does this Riza do?

RIZ  He works in HR.

RUMI  That's not very desi, is it? [**Of Pakistani/Indian/
Bangladeshi origin**]

RIZ  No?

RUMI  Got to be a doctor, lawyer or engineer. Holy trinity of
brown people professions.

RIZ  Well, Riza isn't. He's a coconut too. Go on, introduce
yourself.

RUMI  To who?

   RIZ *enters.*

RIZ  Riza.

   *He holds out his hand for* RUMI, *who hesitates but then
   takes it. They shake.*

RUMI  Rumi.

RIZA  Like the poet?

RUMI  Yeah, just like him.

RIZA  Pretty.

RUMI  Thank you!

RIZA  What do you do?

RUMI  I'm a food blogger.

RIZA  No way! That's awesome. Do you get to go to fancy places?

RUMI  This feels weird.

RIZ  (*as himself*) Keep going, doing just fine.

RUMI  But—

RIZA  Any celebrity chef encounters?

RUMI  I once met Michel Roux Junior at Le Gavroche?

RIZA  How was it? I've heard the black pudding is epic!

RUMI  It is.

RIZA  I always get freaked out in restaurants in case someone sees me eating something that's definitely not halal, so I eat really fast, and then I feel like I never get to enjoy my food.

RUMI  Someone once told my mum they saw me in Superdrug buying tampons. / Tampons!

RIZA  / Who has that much spare time on their hands?

RUMI  I see lads from the community smoking all the time, no one calls home on them.

RIZA  The patriarchy hurts Asian men too. I wish my brothers could see how poorly we treat our women and we can work together to... Wait, what's that?

RUMI  What?

RIZA  Do you hear that? That's the sound of—

RUMI  What? I don't hear anything.

RIZA  My carriage! It's turning back into a pumpkin. I – I have to go.

RUMI  What the—

RIZ  You were becoming too attached. A woke brown dude who encourages *haram* food choices? Doesn't exist. And even if he does, you won't find him tonight. [**Not permitted in Islam**]

RUMI  He'll be there. The guy who's equally as uncomfortable as me. He's probably there because some family member forced him to be. I'll just approach him at the bar later and come clean. We'll hit it off, we can go for an actual date and everything, everything will be okay.

RIZ  Unless there's no bar.

RUMI  Shit. There's not going to be a bar, is there?

*Blackout.*

## Scene Two

*Lights snap up on* **RUMI** *in a pub in London, propping up the bar, wearing her full abaya and headscarf. She's drunk and having an aggressive conversation with herself.* **SIMON** *watches, concerned.*

**RUMI**  I told you. But...you don't... Think you know—

Can't believe you thought... Was not the best – not the – the worst idea—

*Beat.*

You, Rumi, are an absolute, complete—

Fazool. [**stupid**]

Yes! That's exactly what you are.

And you just had to bring up...

Have you got any pork scratchings?

*A beat.*

Beef jerky?

What kind of establishment is this?

Fuck, it's hot.

Is there air-con?

Sweating so much, it's...so. Fuck.

*As* **RUMI** *begins fanning herself and dramatically wiping sweat away,* **SIMON** *approaches.*

**SIMON**  Are you okay?

**RUMI**  Are *you* okay?

**SIMON**  Do you want to go outside?

**RUMI**  What?

**SIMON**  Get some air. Cool off...

**RUMI**  Who are you?

**SIMON**  You look like you're / not having a...

**RUMI**  / Like what?

**SIMON**  ...Sweaty. Uncomfortable. Distressed.

**RUMI**  Are you calling me a terrorist?

**SIMON**  What?

**RUMI**  Do you go around accusing every brown girl of being a terrorist?

**SIMON**  No, / not at all!

**RUMI**  / I'm not even that brown you know. / People think I'm Italian.

**SIMON**  / I wasn't implying—

**RUMI**  / Or Brazilian. I'VE BEEN TOLD, I'M NOT EVEN THAT BROWN.

**SIMON**  Do you want me to phone someone?

**RUMI**  I'm just sitting here. Standing here, making some important life decisions, and – and you – you – you're all like—

**SIMON**  What?

*A beat.* **RUMI** *looks at* **SIMON** *and then she remembers she's still wearing her abaya.*

**RUMI**  Just being nice. You are being nice because I'm... I'm still... *(She gestures to her abaya.)* And, and... What a fucking mess.

**SIMON**  I don't think anyone noticed.

**RUMI**  Owwwhh and I was having that conversation—

**SIMON**  With yourself.

**RUMI**  With myself. Absolute dickhead.

**SIMON**  I think you got away with it.

**RUMI** Fuck.

**SIMON** I don't see any men in white coats so...

*A pause.*

**RUMI** What's the worst decision you've ever made?

**SIMON** Me?

**RUMI** Ever done something you thought could potentially change your entire life? But then you realise you've actually momentously misjudged the situation and ended up wishing you'd never had the bloody idea in the first place?

**SIMON** ...

**RUMI** No?

**SIMON** Maybe—

**RUMI** I went halal speed dating tonight.

**SIMON** That's a thing?

**RUMI** Apparently.

**SIMON** And it...?

**RUMI** Did not go well. Clearly...

**SIMON** Are you allowed to date?

**RUMI** We're not all married off at sixteen. I mean, it would have been easier if my parents had arranged something.

> **RUMI** *starts to take off her abaya, but leaves her head covered.* **SIMON** *stares.*

But I'm too difficult. I wouldn't even have minded if they'd packed me off to the motherland. I could be married to some mountain village chief by now, with a herd of goats, spending my days drinking masala chai and frolicking in the Himalayas. Means I wouldn't have to do crap like this.

**SIMON** Should you be taking that off? In front of me?

RUMI  I think being in a pub, twatted, negates anything this might represent. And avert your dirty male gaze, or I'll have to put it back on.

SIMON  Didn't think Muslims were allowed to drink.

RUMI  They're not. That's like Islam 101. Along with no bacon and sex before marriage. Boring bastards.

SIMON  So you're not Muslim?

RUMI  Didn't say that.

SIMON  But—

RUMI  It's almost like I'm a complex human being with different layers of cultural identity and can't be categorised by the colour of my skin or the religion of my parents, that I may or may not choose to follow.

SIMON  Right.

RUMI  I'm Muslim in the same way you're probably Christian.

SIMON  Catholic. And I'm not really, my mum—

RUMI  Exactly. I mean, I stand up for Islam all the time, it's this thing that I do. Every time I see, or hear, Islamophobia, I get all angry and start calling everyone an ignorant bigot and make a scene. Just yesterday, on the Tube I saw this dude and he pushed a woman in a hijab who was holding a baby and I was ready for a ruckus.

SIMON  I can imagine.

RUMI  But whenever I have to fill out the census I freeze. Never know which box to tick. Can't really be a Muslim if you don't follow any of the rules...?

SIMON  They're all the same though, aren't they? All got lots of rules and only one god. As long as you believe in him, you'll be alright.

RUMI  Or her.

SIMON  Or her.

*Pause.*

Well. Shit got deep.

**RUMI** Yeah.

**SIMON** Want a drink?

**RUMI** I should probably go home and bury my dignity in a box in the garden.

**SIMON** Consider a burial at sea, into a pint? Night's still young.

**RUMI** What time is it?

**SIMON** No idea. I don't subscribe to social constructs like time! Friday nights are for—

**RUMI** I bet you're one of those people who doesn't see colour.

**SIMON** Totally colourblind. Equal opportunity pessimist, everyone's shit, and then you die.

**RUMI** I prefer, "Don't be a dick, and then you die."

**SIMON** Write that next time you have to fill out a form.

**RUMI** Are you here on your own?

**SIMON** No. *(beat)* Yes. I stopped in for one before checking in on my mum.

**RUMI** And then you got sucked into my existential crisis.

**SIMON** Something to do.

**RUMI** Fine. One drink.

**SIMON** How about dinner instead? I know a great Indian place.

**RUMI** No, you don't.

**SIMON** It's really good—

**RUMI** No. No, it's not.

**SIMON** Come see for yourself. That's if you, do you date...?

*A gesture.*

RUMI Depends.

SIMON On?

RUMI How d'you feel about converting to Islam?

SIMON Buy me a biryani and I'm up for anything.

RUMI ...

SIMON *holds out his hand for* RUMI.

SIMON I'm Simon.

RUMI *takes it.*

RUMI Rumi.

SIMON Pleased to meet you.

RUMI Don't tell anyone but I am rather partial to a chicken tikka masala.

SIMON My lips are sealed.

*As they get up to leave,* SIMON *gestures to* RUMI's *hijab.*

Are you going to take that off?

RUMI Nope. Hijab hair. It's a no-go.

SIMON You're alright if we check in on my mum? It's on the way.

RUMI You know white people can be Muslim too.

Culture and religion are different. Plus I never said I don't date non-Muslims.

SIMON You went halal speed dating.

RUMI Because I'm open to dating everyone. Not everyone. I'm not... I'm open to all men. Not all men—

SIMON Shall we?

RUMI Yes.

*Lights fade.*

## Scene Three

*We are back in* RIZ*'s world as she is putting the final touches to her hair, preparing for a date with* SIMON. *Lights rise on* RUMI *staring into the audience as if into a mirror.* RIZ *speaks, as if from nowhere.*

RIZ  No more goras, we said. [**white boys**]

RUMI  *You* said. Plus his face gives me a ladyboner. So.

RIZ  What about Riza?

RUMI  He doesn't exist.

RIZ  You haven't looked.

RUMI  Been busy.

RIZ  Busy texting fuckboys.

RUMI  Simon is not a fuckboy.

RIZ  He might not be a fuckboy, but is he ready for brown-girl drama?

RUMI  It's just a date.

RIZ  How many dates until it's super-serious and we can't get out of it?

RUMI  Why would I want to get out of it?

RIZ  Because, and I quote, "I just want someone to watch old Bollywood movies with and eat chaat with. I don't want to have to translate everything at family dinners."

RUMI  Want to try your luck at halal speed dating again?

RIZ  Hell no. That's the saddest we've ever been. Never speak of that again.

RUMI  So...?

*A pause whilst* RIZ *considers their options.*

RIZ  Theek hai gee. [**fine**]

**RUMI** ...

**RIZ** But don't say I didn't warn you.

**RUMI** As if you'd let me forget.

*Lights fade.*

## Scene Four

*RUMI and SIMON are on a date at a golf putting range.
Lights rise on RUMI sulking, she's losing.*

RUMI  I didn't realise you were this competitive.

SIMON  I'm not.

RUMI  You just listed all the medals you've won since primary school—

SIMON  It's important that you know I am very accomplished despite not having formal qualifications.

*SIMON swings and watches his ball.*

I'm still five points ahead!

RUMI  Rub it in.

*RUMI takes a swing. From her reaction we see it wasn't a good shot.*

SIMON  Your swing's off.

RUMI  You think?

SIMON  Try sticking your butt out a bit.

RUMI  Excuse me?

SIMON  Like this.

*He demonstrates. RUMI tries but it's not right.*

Here. Let me.

*He puts his arms around RUMI to help her with her form, they're close, it's surprisingly comfortable.*

Keep looking at the ball...bend knees, swing and...

*They stay close, watching the ball.*

Ah. Well.

**RUMI** See. Not my thing.

**SIMON** You've managed to hold onto the club though, last time I brought someone here they let go and the club went flying. Almost hit a hen party.

**RUMI** Ohhhh. So this is your spot.

**SIMON** What?

**RUMI** And there I was thinking I was special. But no, I'm just part of a long line of ladies that get treated to a quick grope under the guise of high-end golf training.

**SIMON** The last time was three years ago!

**RUMI** Whatever.

**SIMON** Seriously. I was so traumatised by it that I just stopped dating. Flat out gave up women.

**RUMI** That's nothing. I once went on a date with a guy who had given up all sexual contact for Lent. He wouldn't even hug me goodbye.

> **SIMON** *swings again, it's a good shot and he tries to down play it.*

**SIMON** Now who's being competitive?

**RUMI** ...

**SIMON** What about once Lent was over?

**RUMI** He shook my hand.

**SIMON** Fool!

**RUMI** I thought there was something so wrong with me I went into hiding for six months.

**SIMON** His loss is my gain.

**RUMI** It most certainly is.

> *A moment between them and then it's* **RUMI***'s turn. She half-heartedly swings and they both watch the ball flop. She's disappointed.*

SIMON  I offered to take you bowling.

RUMI  I'm shit at that too. Sports are not my thing.

SIMON  What is your thing?

RUMI  Food. Booze. Long walks along the beach. I'm a simple creature.

SIMON  Next time I'll just take you to Spain.

RUMI  Spain?

SIMON  Or Southend. Both have beaches.

RUMI  Okay. So. I... This is silly but... I have this innate fear that if I leave the country something will happen to me, and then whoever I'm with will have to call home and tell my parents, and then they'll realise that I've lied to them and it will open a massive can of worms and I'll be found out as some heathen devil child. Especially if I'm away with a boy.

SIMON  Southend it is. *(beat)* They must know what you get up to?

RUMI  Probably. Maybe. Don't know. My mum's a fiend and somehow always finds out.

SIMON  Wouldn't it be easier if you were just honest?

RUMI  It's about respect. I live at home and so I have to... moderate. You know?

SIMON  I thought my mother was difficult.

SIMON *swings. It's a good one. He calculates his score.*

You could still win.

RUMI  How is she at the moment?

SIMON  As well as can be expected. I try and get her out of the house at least once a week but we didn't manage it during the week and today I'm, well, I'm here so she's a little cranky.

RUMI  We could have postponed.

SIMON  No, I...

**RUMI** I wanted to see you too.

*Pause.*

**SIMON** Is it easier when you date Asian or Muslim guys then?

**RUMI** I have never dated a brown boy.

**SIMON** Never?

**RUMI** Not really, not properly.

**SIMON** You're attracted to a pasty complexion?

**RUMI** It's not that, just...the Pakistani guys I've liked have always opted for white women.

**SIMON** You were meant to say, "You're not pasty."

**RUMI** Sorry. You're not pasty.

**SIMON** Once more with feeling.

**RUMI** You have a lovely colouring.

**SIMON** Sounds like something you'd say to a child that's used crayon outside of the lines.

**RUMI** *goes to take her turn but then spots someone.*

**RUMI** Simon. I don't mean to alarm you but—

**SIMON** What?

**RUMI** I really need you to come over here, right now.

**SIMON** What?

**RUMI** *grabs* **SIMON** *and buries her face in his chest. She spins him so they're facing the other way.*

**RUMI** Just act normal.

**SIMON** A little difficult when you're trying to burrow into my chest.

**SIMONS** *tries to pry her off him, she grabs on tighter.*

Rumi!

RUMI  Just a second. I'm just checking everything...

SIMON *is completely bemused until he realises.*

SIMON  Have you seen someone you know?

RUMI  With the red hat.

SIMON  He's leaving.

*They wait.* SIMON *smiles and nods to somone who's obviously watching them.*

Okay, they're gone.

RUMI  Shit. Shit.

SIMON  That was really embarrassing.

RUMI  Do you think he saw?

SIMON  Are you ashamed of me?

RUMI  I panicked.

SIMON  Are you going to do this every time we're in public?

RUMI  Probably, unless you're up for a fake tan and a mullah beard. And then I can pass you off as a Phattan, Pushtun, Persian whatever, you know the guys that live in the Northern Frontier.

SIMON  ...

RUMI  Near Afghanistan?

SIMON  ...

RUMI  Where you can't go anymore, because...

SIMON  ...

RUMI  The Taliban basically.

SIMON  I've won. So, game's over. You can go.

*A long pause.*

RUMI  I don't want to leave it like this.

**SIMON**  It's fine. You got to do what you got to do.

**RUMI**  I can't...can't risk...until I know / what this is.

**SIMON**  / It's fine. Really.

*Beat.*

**RUMI**  Okay.

**SIMON**  Okay.

*He touches her lightly, a gesture of reassurance.*

*Lights fade.*

## Scene Five

*Lights up on* RUMI, *facing the audience, as if into a mirror. She is doing her make-up but* RIZ *keeps sabotaging her progress.*

RIZ  You are pushing our luck.

RUMI  I've been more careful.

RIZ  It is just a matter of time until this all explodes in our face. And not in a good way.

RUMI  I've got it under control. *(beat)* He's started watching *Goodness Gracious Me.*

RIZ  Oh great. When he finally meets ma he'll present her with a small aubergine.

RUMI  And thrust it at her like Rafiki holds Simba off the edge of the cliff at the beginning of *The Lion King.*

RIZ  Making him brown won't make up for *your* lack of brownness—

RUMI  Just because I don't hang out with other brown people and / don't listen to brown music...

RIZ  / And insist on doing everything differently.

RUMI  ...Or watch Bollywood movies doesn't mean that I'm ashamed of my skin colour.

RIZ  ...

RUMI  My Urdu's actually pretty good.

RIZ  Teri punjabi shit hain. [**Your Punjabi needs work**]

RUMI  Being a coconut doesn't make me a bad person.

RIZ  Didn't say that.

RUMI  It was implied.

RIZ  By every other person in the community.

RUMI  Don't care about them.

RIZ  Maybe we should?

RUMI  What's more important? Someone with the right vocabulary and skin colour, or real, actual love?

RIZ  ...

RUMI*'s done and ready to leave.*

RUMI  Anything useful to add?

RIZ  Imagine ma's face when you bring Simon home. What will you say? What words will you use to break her heart?

RUMI  I'll just say...

RIZ  Yes?

RUMI  Ma. *(pause)* This. Um. I know... You know me, that I'm... I've got news. I...

*Silence. She can't.*

*Blackout.*

## Scene Six

*Lights up on* SIMON *leading a blindfolded* RUMI *onto the stage. He has set up a picnic with a basket of food and cans of cocktail. There are blankets and it's all very cosy.* SIMON *removes* RUMI'*s blindfold.*

SIMON Ta-dah!

RUMI Wow. This is—

SIMON The last few times I've seen you it's been... So I wanted us to be able to enjoy time together properly. Alone. No stress.

RUMI Shit. You *are* a serial killer.

SIMON Too late if I am. No one here for miles.

RUMI This is very sweet of you.

*They sit and get comfortable with the blankets.* SIMON *hands* RUMI *a drink. They drink in silence for a moment.*

I feel like we should have a telescope or...

SIMON No need. There's the pan. You see? *(He points.)* And follow its handle and...there. There's the North Star. I think that one's Jupiter.

RUMI Who knew you were such an astronomer.

*Beat.*

SIMON What do you think is out there?

RUMI Space dust and little green men.

SIMON There's got to be something else.

RUMI Does there?

SIMON They say there's forty billion planets that are *just* as habitable as Earth, just in our galaxy. Makes me think that anything's possible. If not here, then on one of those other planets. Out there, there's another Simon who's maybe had better options in his life.

*Pause. They stare.*

RUMI  What's alternative Simon doing right now?

SIMON  Hanging out with alternative Rumi.

RUMI  You think?

SIMON  Yeah. Except on that planet he's the one that wears the pants.

RUMI  Alternative Rumi is a celebrity chef so she needs alternative Simon to take charge, that's why.

SIMON  Chef is too close to food blogger. Alternative Rumi has to be something completely different.

RUMI  A fearless adventurer that's travelled across the galaxy.

SIMON  I think you're brave.

RUMI  Even though I'm too scared to step completely out of the box here? Don't know where I fit, but don't know how to find out.

SIMON  Alternative Simon wants a quiet life. He's so busy every day with his fancy job where he's terribly important and does life-saving work that he really just craves peace and quiet.

*They lie down on the blankets, staring.*

RUMI  Are you looking for a new job?

SIMON  Yes. No. I don't think I can take just another job.

RUMI  So don't. Travel the world. Alternative Simon can come over here and deal with your life. Or not. Time for you to take a chance.

SIMON  Bit hypocritical of you.

RUMI  Get some carers and book a flight.

SIMON  Are you trying to get rid of me?

RUMI  No. I—

SIMON  Where is this headed?

**RUMI** What?

**SIMON** You've been holding back since the moment we met and now you want me to piss off around the world.

**RUMI** I—

**SIMON** We can barely go out without you jumping at the sight of every... It's always one eye over your shoulder.

**RUMI** I have a lot of aunties, okay.

**SIMON** Come away with me.

**RUMI** What?

**SIMON** You're right. I should go. Seize the day, but I want to do it with you.

**RUMI** I can't go away with you.

**SIMON** Why not?

**RUMI** What will I say to my parents?

**SIMON** Tell them the truth.

**RUMI** They'd have heart attacks! Or worse—

**SIMON** What, what would they actually do?

**RUMI** ...

**SIMON** You're funny and sweet and kind. You're not a bad person.

**RUMI** ...

**SIMON** All my eggs are in your basket so—

**RUMI** You'll need to convert.

**SIMON** What?

**RUMI** I did tell you. The first time we met. Not my fault you didn't take it seriously.

**SIMON** I heard you. I just didn't think...

**RUMI** Well that's what it takes. I can't without—

**SIMON** My mum—

RUMI  My mum!

SIMON  You've spent six months convincing me you're not interested in your religion and now you want to force it on me?

RUMI  I'm not forcing. And it's not about religion, it's...

SIMON  What?

RUMI  Take it or leave it.

SIMON  You'd give this up? Us?

RUMI  I don't want to.

SIMON  So why then?

RUMI  To save face. To heal hearts. For an easy life. Because I couldn't imagine it any other way. To show I am not a colossal fuck-up.

SIMON  Being with me makes you a fuck up?

RUMI  No – a relationship in the open has to be marriage / and for that you have to convert.

SIMON  / Marriage?

RUMI  Just an Islamic one—

SIMON  What the actual fuck?

RUMI  Everyone does it. Doesn't mean anything.

SIMON  Oh great, a meaningless marriage, / just what every man wants.

RUMI  / I don't mean meaningless, of course it's...

SIMON  ...

RUMI  I love you. *(pause)* And it's—

SIMON  I love you too.

*Pause.*

Fucking parents.

**RUMI** ...

**SIMON** I don't want to lose you, but—

**RUMI** But?

**SIMON** I don't know.

*They embrace, staring at the stars in silence.*

*Lights fade.*

## Scene Seven

*We are at* SIMON's *mother's wake. Lights rise on* RUMI *and* SIMON *at the bar, he's exhausted but okay.*

RUMI  She'd be proud of you.

SIMON  I should have done more. At the end.

RUMI  You couldn't. No family, few friends—

SIMON  She spent five years in bed and I can't remember the last time someone came to visit. I should have called, made sure she had someone.

RUMI  I'm here now and I'm ready to celebrate her memory. She hated me but...

SIMON  She didn't hate you.

RUMI  Just wished you'd chosen a nice white girl.

SIMON  No—

RUMI  Did you tell her I know every king of England since Henry the Eighth?

SIMON  I even tried to explain the concept of a coconut, but she wasn't used to me giving a shit about anything. Thought you were distracting me from—

RUMI  From what?

SIMON  Job, life, money. Thought I was changing too much.

RUMI  I don't want you to—

SIMON  I am changing though. It's a good thing. You make me better, Rumi. It's a shame she couldn't see that.

RUMI  ...

SIMON  I'm ready to start living, a good life.

RUMI  Okay.

**SIMON** I'll do whatever. Whatever you need for us to be legit, halal, as they say.

**RUMI** Are you sure?

**SIMON** Tomorrow, let's go to the mosque—

**RUMI** You know you don't need to change who you are. The conversion, it's only in principle. I won't wake up forty years down the line and suddenly want to be a super-Muslim.

**SIMON** ...

**RUMI** I'll still get my boobs out every once in a while. Just saying.

**SIMON** Promise?

**RUMI** Promise. But you'll have to say a prayer.

**SIMON** Prayer?

**RUMI** A short prayer. Not even a prayer, as such.

**SIMON** Right.

**RUMI** It's a declaration. A short declaration. The declaration of faith—

Just...in the mosque.

**SIMON** A mosque?

**RUMI** In front of—

**SIMON** In public?

**RUMI** Only an imaam. Not – not like the whole Muslim Council of England. Just you, me and the imaam.

**SIMON** Okay.

**RUMI** And my parents, cos you know – oh and maybe my auntie.

**SIMON** Auntie?

**RUMI** No. No aunties.

**SIMON** Sure?

**RUMI** One auntie, that's all.

**SIMON** Cannot wait.

**RUMI** And don't worry about circumcision, I'll take care of that. Not take care of that, you know. Not with scissors.

**SIMON** I get it.

**RUMI** You sure about this?

**SIMON** What's going to happen?

**RUMI** The imaam will just ask you a couple of questions, mostly about your intentions, you'll repeat the declaration of faith after him and that's that.

**SIMON** That's it?

**RUMI** That's it.

**SIMON** What if he asks me questions about Islam?

**RUMI** He just wants to know that you're serious.

**SIMON** I'd do anything for you.

> **SIMON** *kisses* **RUMI.**

**RUMI** I'm here for you.

**SIMON** I'm glad.

**RUMI** Me too.

> *Lights fade.*

## Scene Eight

*Lights snap up on* **SIMON** *and* **IRFAN** *sitting in the mosque.* **SIMON** *is way out of his depth.*

**IRFAN**  Did you grow up with religion, Simon?

**SIMON**  Sort of. My mum was Catholic. I had communion, I've attended plenty of masses.

**IRFAN**  But?

**SIMON**  But nothing. I just wouldn't consider myself a Catholic.

**IRFAN**  But you're ready to call yourself a Muslim?

**SIMON**  Yes—

**IRFAN**  Have you been interested in Islam long?

**SIMON**  A while.

**IRFAN**  Are you in a relationship with Rumi?

   **SIMON** *considers lying to* **IRFAN**.

**SIMON**  Yes.

**IRFAN**  You know that is haram?

**SIMON**  Yes, that's why we want to, um, you know, legitimise things.

**IRFAN**  Is she practising?

**SIMON**  Her family are all... It's important to them.

**IRFAN**  Does she support your decision?

**SIMON**  They—

**IRFAN**  Does *she*?

**SIMON**  Yes.

**IRFAN**  Is Islam important to you, Simon?

**SIMON**  It is becoming very important.

IRFAN  Because you want to marry Rumi?

SIMON  Not just—

IRFAN  You want to become a Muslim so you can get married?

SIMON  ...

IRFAN  Would you still want to be a Muslim if it wasn't for her?

SIMON  ...

IRFAN  Because mortal relationships are unsteady. Humans are
fickle. But Allah, Allah is steadfast. Your relationship with
him must be solid before you embrace Islam. Before you
jump into a marriage. Do you understand?

SIMON  Yes.

IRFAN  Tell me what you know about Islam.

SIMON  Okay. Uh. Well, there are five pillars.

IRFAN  Can you name them?

SIMON  ...

IRFAN  Zakat. That's one. Do you know what that is?

SIMON  Could you repeat the word?

IRFAN  That's charity. You pay 2 per cent of your yearly savings
to charity.

SIMON  Yes! I know that. And there's the one, the pilgrimage.
Every year. You wear the, the um—

IRFAN  That's hajj. What else? What do Muslims think about
alcohol?

SIMON  Excuse me?

IRFAN  Are you a big drinker, a party goer?

SIMON  No.

IRFAN  Then the transition, after today, will be easier. Tell me
the first pillar of Islam.

**SIMON** I know that one. It's—

**IRFAN** Yes?

**SIMON** The declaration of faith.

**IRFAN** The shahada.

**SIMON** It means I submit.

**IRFAN** And do you?

**SIMON** I do.

*A pause.* **SIMON** *is shit-scared.*

**IRFAN** I want you to attend some classes.

**SIMON** Classes?

**IRFAN** Simon, you strike me as someone with a good heart, and embracing a whole new religion is a big sacrifice to make for someone you love. But too many people are unprepared for this journey they are embarking on. I want both of you to learn to love your faith, together.

**SIMON** I can't speak for Rumi, but I—

**IRFAN** Once you are married, you will be her guide, Simon. You have to care for, and protect Rumi. You can't do that without a solid understanding of your religion. I expect you to study, to converse with me on a regular basis, to promise to stay focused. It's non-negotiable.

**SIMON** I—

**IRFAN** Can you do that?

**SIMON** ...

**IRFAN** It's a new start. Everything that came before is before—

**SIMON** Okay.

**IRFAN** Not just for her?

**SIMON** Of course for her, but also for me.

**IRFAN**  I'm glad to hear it.

**SIMON**  Thank you. Thank you for this.

*They shake hands and embrace.*

**IRFAN**  Are you ready?

**SIMON**  Yes.

**IRFAN**  Repeat after me.

*Blackout.*


### End of Act One

# ACT TWO

## Scene One

*The stage is set as* **RUMI** *and* **SIMON**'s *flat, somewhere in London. They have been married for a few weeks. Lights rise on* **RUMI** *on the sofa, magazine in hand, busy with the Closer crossword.*

**SIMON** *calls from offstage:*

**SIMON**  Babe?

**RUMI**  Yes?

**SIMON**  Why are Muslims so obsessed with hair?

**RUMI**  What?

**SIMON**  Hair.

*SIMON enters wearing a thobe.* **RUMI** *doesn't notice.*

Why are Muslims so obsessed with hair? I thought Sikhs were but...

**RUMI**  ...

*SIMON moves closer to* **RUMI**. *Swishing his thobe, hoping to make her notice him.*

**SIMON**  Apparently you can have a beard but not a moustache.

*RUMI looks up and sees* **SIMON** *in the thobe. She has to hold in her laughter. He's distracted by the sight of himself in the mirror.*

**RUMI**  Where, um, where...where did you find that titbit of info?

*He continues swishing the thobe around.*

**SIMON**  A website. Any query you have, just type it in and, voila, a legitimate scholar answers.

**RUMI**  What did you google to get there?

**SIMON**  Something like why do Muslims have beards.

**RUMI**  Why do Muslims have beards?

**SIMON**  Because it's manly. I could pull one off? Right?

**RUMI**  Mmmhmmmm.

*Frustrated,* **SIMON** *grabs the Closer magazine off* **RUMI** *and checks her progress. She holds out her hand, waiting for him to give it back. He doesn't.*

**SIMON**  This one's wrong.

**RUMI**  Which one.

**SIMON**  *This one.*

**RUMI**  That's very helpful, because you know, I can absolutely see which one you're pointing too.

**SIMON**  Picture D is not Kim Kardashian.

**RUMI**  So who is it?

**SIMON**  For someone who watches so much trash TV, you're not very good at this.

**RUMI**  Are you being a dick because I didn't say anything about your dress?

**SIMON**  My thobe *(He pronounces it "Thobey")*

**RUMI**  Your what?

**SIMON**  It's not a dress.

**RUMI**  What did you call it?

**SIMON**  Thobey.

**RUMI**  It's pronounced "Thobe".

**SIMON**  Is it?

**RUMI**  Yes.

**SIMON**  Are you sure?

**RUMI**  Why are you wearing it?

**SIMON**  Guy on Green Street called it a thobey.

**RUMI**  It's a thobe.

**SIMON**  Thobey.

**RUMI**  Thobe.

**SIMON**  Thobe.

**RUMI**  Yes.

**SIMON**  Really?

**RUMI**  WHY ARE YOU WEARING THE THOBE?

*Beat.*

**SIMON**  You went all fundo there for a moment.

**RUMI**  Fundo?

**SIMON**  It means fundamentalist, you told me that.

**RUMI**  I know what fundo means. I'm a bloody Muslamic.

**SIMON**  I can use all those words now. I'm a bloody Muslamic too. And I've got a thobey to prove it.

**RUMI**  So I see.

**SIMON**  I think it makes me look regal.

**RUMI**  You look like an albino African prince. Sort of like Eddie Murphy in *Coming to America*.

**SIMON**  Great movie.

**RUMI**  When are you going to wear it, in your day-to-day life?

**SIMON**  To Jummah. [**Friday prayers**]

**RUMI**  You're going to the mosque?

**SIMON**  I have to meet Irfan.

**RUMI**  The imaam?

**SIMON**  I've been reading the literature he gave me. And that got me thinking that it was good of him to agree to marry us, and I should probably thank him.

**RUMI**  So send him an email.

**SIMON**  I did.

**RUMI**  And?

**SIMON**  He told me to come in for a chat.

**RUMI**  Right.

   *Beat.*

**SIMON**  I want to experience praying. There's something really powerful about watching a group of people do the same thing with real intent and passion.

**RUMI**  Watch synchronised swimming!

**SIMON**  When's the last time you prayed?

**RUMI**  You don't know the words.

**SIMON**  I know the actions.

**RUMI**  It's not yoga! You can't just do the movement and mumble along beside them.

   *A pause.*

**SIMON**  Irfan's a nice guy. He's giving me a chance.

**RUMI**  At what?

**SIMON**  To prove myself.

**RUMI**  You don't need to. Everyone's happy you're making a concerted effort to learn more Urdu.

**SIMON**  "Could you pass the chicken curry" hasn't got quite the gravitas I was hoping for.

RUMI  Hey, everyone fights over my grandma's tomato chicken. That's a key phrase you've mastered.

SIMON  I've been summoned.

RUMI  Babe, you survived a trip to Tayyabs with my entire family *and* you know who Aishwarya Rai is, that's good enough for me.

SIMON  I'm curious, what's the harm?

RUMI  Just master the art of bhangra and we're sorted.

SIMON  Come with me.

RUMI  No.

SIMON  Two infidels are better than one.

RUMI  He's not interested in what I have to say.

SIMON  I'd feel better with you there.

RUMI  It's my day off.

SIMON  Half an hour, that's all.

*A pause.*

RUMI  Fine. But please take off that thobe. No one's going to take you seriously.

SIMON  No way. I'm wearing it everywhere.

RUMI  Please no.

SIMON  Come on. Don't want to be late.

RUMI  Yeah, give me a minute, got to grab a scarf.

SIMON *exits the room, swishing his thobe.* RUMI *falls into the sofa.*

*Lights fade.*

## Scene Two

*Friday after Jummah prayers. Lights rise on* **SIMON** *and* **RUMI** *in the mosque, waiting for* **IRFAN**. *He enters.*

**IRFAN**  As-salamu alaykum. Simon, Rumi.

**SIMON**  Thank you so much for seeing us.

**IRFAN**  That's okay, you are always very welcome here. Would you like some tea?

**RUMI**  No, thank you.

**IRFAN**  How are you both?

**SIMON**  We're doing well.

**IRFAN**  Rumi?

**RUMI**  Yeah, good mashallah.

**IRFAN**  Mashallah. Settling into married life?

**SIMON**  Yes.

**IRFAN**  Good. Navigating cultural differences okay?

**RUMI**  Fine.

*Pause.*

**IRFAN**  Right, well I asked you to come in because we offer a range of classes, especially for converts and newly-weds, and I think the two of you could benefit from spending some time at the mosque, in the company of other couples like yourselves.

**RUMI**  Like us?

**SIMON**  You mean mixed race? Or new to the mosque?

**IRFAN**  Every couple is different, we just want to ensure that you're on the same page in terms of knowledge of Islam, / both theoretically and in practice.

RUMI  / I have quite a good base knowledge and Simon, obviously—

SIMON  I'd really like to learn the basics first. On my own.

RUMI  What?

IRFAN  We really do encourage couples to actively participate in each other's learning. It's much easier when there are two of you, much like life.

RUMI  I can do that at home—

SIMON  She *already* knows all this stuff, so if I need to...I can—

IRFAN  It is very important that you engage with each other, and the mosque every week. At least for the first year.

RUMI  Year?

SIMON  I want to do this.

RUMI  Simon—

SIMON  For myself. Get my head around everything.

IRFAN  I offer private classes for adults, in small groups or one to one.

SIMON  I don't even know how to read Arabic.

IRFAN  The children that attend our Sunday school are quite multicultural. Not all of them grow up with Arabic in the house.

SIMON  So they're learning from scratch too?

IRFAN  At the Sunday school they are, yes.

RUMI  You don't want to join that—

SIMON  I could.

IRFAN  The Sunday school?

SIMON  That would be great.

RUMI  Simon, only young people attend the sessions on Sunday.

SIMON   That's fine. I'll be at the same level.

IRFAN   Practising Islam as an adult is very different. I feel it would be more appropriate that you learn as you go along, within context of your day-to-day *adult* life.

SIMON   I'd really like to start at the beginning. I want to get it right.

RUMI   Babe—

IRFAN   If you're sure.

SIMON   I am.

IRFAN   I can't fault your enthusiasm, Simon. I guess we will see you on Sunday. And, Rumi—

RUMI   I'll come by next Friday.

IRFAN   Make sure you do.

SIMON   As-salamu alaykum.

IRFAN   Wa-alaykum as salam. Excuse me, I have something to attend to.

> IRFAN *and* SIMON *shake hands,* IRFAN *exits.*

RUMI   What the actual fuck?

SIMON   You can't swear in a mosque!

RUMI   "I'd really like to start at the beginning"?

SIMON   I would.

RUMI   What's up with the sudden interest in Islam?

SIMON   I made a declaration.

RUMI   So now you're all thobes and salaams?

SIMON   I was being polite.

RUMI   And Sunday school?

SIMON   I promised myself I'd take things seriously. Fix up, start acting worthy.

**RUMI** You are more than worthy, Simon. You are lovely.

**SIMON** I want to build something solid and stable for us.

**RUMI** Okay. *(beat)* But Sundays are for boozy brunches, yeah, not kiddy school.

**SIMON** Don't call it that.

**RUMI** Seriously though...?

**SIMON** Yeah, okay.

**RUMI** Okay.

*Lights down.*

## Scene Three

*Lights rise on* **RUMI** *and* **SIMON** *in the kitchen, laying the table for dinner. Their conversation is fun and playful.*

**SIMON**  So that's why cropped trousers are sunnah. [**the way of the prophet peace be upon him**]

**RUMI**  Do you think God really cares about the length of men's trousers?

**SIMON**  Apparently so.

**RUMI**  Are you sure you're hanging out with legit Muslims and not just Dalston hipsters?

**SIMON**  Very funny.

**RUMI**  Better check with Irfan. Wouldn't want you to start hacking at your jeans if there's no sawab in it. [**spiritual merit or reward from the performance of good deeds and piety**]

**SIMON**  At least I'll finally be cool.

**RUMI**  At least there's that.

**SIMON**  What's for dinner? Smells great.

**RUMI**  Lasagna. Another twenty minutes though.

**SIMON**  You are a goddess.

**RUMI**  Aren't I just. You okay to make salad? I've got a deadline.

**SIMON**  Go. I have everything under control.

*RUMI exits as* **SIMON** *finishes the table. He goes to the fridge to take out ingredients for a salad and spies bacon tucked away in the back. He is not happy.*

Rumi?

*A pause as he waits for an answer, nothing. He's not happy.*

Is she serious?

Rumi!

There's bacon in the fridge.

**RUMI** *(offstage)* What's that, babe?

**SIMON** Bacon. There's bacon in the fridge. In my fridge.

**RUMI** *(offstage)* Your fridge?

**SIMON** Why is it there? I don't believe you.

> **SIMON** *wants the bacon out of the fridge, but he's unwilling to touch it. He goes to look for a spatula, or some tongs, or anything. Utensils are flying out of cupboards and drawers.*

This is ridiculous. Completely ridiculous.

> **RUMI** *enters, surveys the mess.*

There's bacon in the fridge.

**RUMI** Pre-emptive pork purchasing, for the morning.

**SIMON** But we were just talking about... And—

**RUMI** And what?

**SIMON** Why is it in the fridge? With everything else?

**RUMI** Where else am I meant to put it?

**SIMON** Not here.

**RUMI** It's not for you. You don't have to touch it.

**SIMON** I'm not going to.

> *A standoff.*

I'm taking the time to expand my mind—

**RUMI** At your kiddy class?

**SIMON** Don't.

**RUMI** You're in a class with a bunch of kids, what else am I meant to call it?

SIMON  I'm learning about... This is *your* culture—

RUMI  Religion. / It's different.

SIMON  / Irfan says if I want to achieve my goals, I have to focus—

RUMI  What does Irfan say?

SIMON  Not just Irfan—

RUMI  Not just Irfan?

SIMON  I am on a journey.

RUMI  Journey?

SIMON  And when you do this, this kind of stuff, it blocks the...
It makes me feel like it's pointless.

RUMI  I'm not blocking you—

SIMON  I feel—

RUMI  The bacon in the fridge is not blocking your—

SIMON  The bacon is a metaphor.

RUMI  No, no. The bacon is very real. Let me show you.

SIMON  Can you please, please, get it out of the fridge?

RUMI  You used to love bacon.

SIMON  I just want to be a good person.

RUMI  Not eating pork isn't going to make you a good person.

SIMON  It's a start.

RUMI  You really want this gone?

SIMON  Yes. Please.

    *She takes it out of the fridge.*

    Thank you. Thank you, Rumi. I appreciate—

    RUMI *takes out a pan and starts to cook the bacon.*

    You are a fucking joker.

**RUMI**  Just getting it out of your way.

**SIMON**  That's how you want to play this?

**RUMI**  I never play when it comes to pork, you know that.

**SIMON**  That's just—

**RUMI**  I can wear it as a dress if you prefer. Works for Lady Gaga.

**SIMON**  Seriously?

**RUMI**  Pass the brown sauce, please.

**SIMON**  What the fuck is wrong with you?

> **SIMON** *storms off.* **RUMI** *continues cooking the bacon until it's ready. She makes a sandwich and walks into her space, holding it, smelling it. She stares into the audience as if into a mirror, wondering whether to throw the sandwich away or not.* **RIZ** *enters, staring at* **RUMI** *as she just stands, holding the sandwich.*

**RIZ**  IT'S LIKE HE'S READ THE "DUMMY'S GUIDE TO ISLAM" OR SOMETHING.

**RUMI**  Was wondering when you'd pipe up.

**RIZ**  Have we checked his willy? Is it all still there?

**RUMI**  He just wants to get involved with everything. I could stand to do more of that myself.

**RIZ**  Hanging out at the mosque, chilling with the imaam, totally our jam.

**RUMI**  ...

**RIZ**  We're newly-weds, he should be worshiping us, not actually worshiping.

**RUMI**  He's just trying to fit in.

**RIZ**  It's like our childhood all over again.

**RUMI**  He deserves my support.

**RIZ**  You know he's just doing it to feel a part of something. That's all it is. He's going to join them and leave us behind.

**RUMI** ...

**RIZ**  Are you going to eat that sandwich?

*She hands him the sandwich.*

**RUMI**  No.

*He eats it with glee.*

**RIZ**  It's a good sandwich.

**RUMI**  I can't afford to ruin this.

> **RUMI** *exits, disgusted.* **RIZ** *continues eating.*
>
> *Lights down.*

## Scene Four

*It is* **RUMI** *and* **SIMON**'s *one-year anniversary.* **RUMI** *has spent ages choosing the right restaurant.*

*Lights up on the couple.* **RUMI**'s *glass of champagne is half-full.* **SIMON**'s *glass is empty.*

**RUMI**  A toast.

**SIMON**  ...

**RUMI**  To us.

**SIMON**  Of course.

**RUMI**  Your glass is empty.

**SIMON**  I finished it.

**RUMI**  I'll order you another.

**SIMON**  It's okay.

**RUMI**  You barely touched the last lot.

**SIMON**  The waiter spilt most of it.

**RUMI**  You should have complained.

**SIMON**  We can do without.

**RUMI**  You can't toast with an empty glass.

**SIMON**  I've got water.

**RUMI**  Here, have some of mine.

> **RUMI** *pours some champagne from her glass into* **SIMON**'s.

**SIMON**  ...

*A pause. They cheers and* **RUMI** *drinks.* **SIMON** *takes a sip but doesn't really drink anything.* **RUMI** *stares at him.*

**RUMI**  *(beat)* You're not drinking, are you?

SIMON  No.

RUMI  Why didn't you just say?

SIMON  I shouldn't have to.

RUMI  It's our anniversary!

SIMON  And?

RUMI  I thought you'd make an exception for tonight. It's only one. We're celebrating!

SIMON  You don't need to drink, babe, you're perfectly capable of having a good time without.

RUMI  I—

SIMON  Do you think you have a problem?

RUMI  What? No. I like to drink. I don't need to. It's just a bloody toast. I'm not saying let's get drunk, just drink the drop in your glass so we can—

SIMON  Why?

RUMI  Because I'm asking you to.

SIMON  I'm asking you not to.

*A beat.*

RUMI  I'm normal. Drinking is normal. You're the one that's weird.

SIMON  Weird?

RUMI  Okay, not weird, I didn't mean weird, just that you're taking this too far. / You don't have to do any of this!

SIMON  / If you can't give up, you can just say that.

RUMI  You did the important bit. You made the family happy. I'm happy, even Irfan's happy. You did good. The rest is just a—

SIMON  Some of us take our vows seriously.

RUMI  That's not fair, you know I love you.

SIMON  But not enough to accept that I want this to mean something.

RUMI  It already means something.

SIMON  Not enough to change—

RUMI  I don't want to change.

*Beat.*

SIMON  You know the first time I stepped into a mosque, a place of worship, I lied. To Irfan's face—

RUMI  He knew you didn't / really mean it.

SIMON  / For you.

RUMI  Everyone's partner "converts"—

SIMON  I broke my mum's heart, for you.

RUMI  She was okay towards the end, more accepting—

SIMON  Was she though?

RUMI  You sai—

SIMON  I signed a piece of paper, to say I'm a Muslim, a *Muslim*, for you. And now you won't even accept that I'm trying to follow through. To try and become a better person.

RUMI  You think you're a better person than me?

SIMON  You can't make the effort to live a modest—

RUMI  Modest?

SIMON  Modest, fruitful, wholesome life.

RUMI  Where is this coming from?

SIMON  Are you content wasting your life?

RUMI  I'm not wasting—

SIMON  How's the blogging going?

RUMI  What's that got to do with anything?

**SIMON**  Phone ringing off the hook, is it? *Guardian* sent over a big fat advance, have they?

**RUMI**  Two hundred more followers than when we first met!

**SIMON**  Is there any point though?

**RUMI**  It's what I love!

**SIMON**  More than me?

**RUMI**  Simon—

**SIMON**  You need something to focus on, to really make something of yourself.

**RUMI**  ...

**SIMON**  Some direction—

**RUMI**  I've done fucking well. Everything I've achieved—

**SIMON**  Yes and I know you, you can do better.

**RUMI**  ...

**SIMON**  I want more for us... I want you to be a good woman. A good wife.

**RUMI**  I am a bloody good—

**SIMON**  I need some commitment from you. You owe me that at least.

**RUMI**  Owe you?

**SIMON**  I'm trying to sort my life out. I've embraced a new—

**RUMI**  I never asked—

**SIMON**  That's my point. You take everything for granted, everything I've done to be with you, the sacrifice...you're so spoilt. Everyone knows it, everyone says—

**RUMI**  What? / What everyone?

**SIMON**  / You're selfish. / Fucking selfish.

**RUMI**  You better not be talking to randoms about—

**SIMON** Not randoms. The community. *Your* community. Men, and women we meet every week. People who care about us. I never had that. Now I'm part of something and I want to support you, the way they're supporting me and you...you just ignore it. I'm more involved at the mosque than you are. I make more of an effort than you do. It's embarrassing. Why don't you start respecting yourself a bit more, yeah?

*A beat.*

I'm only saying these things because I care. You don't need this. You're better than this.

*He pours* **RUMI***'s drink onto the floor. She looks on in disbelief.*

I believe in you.

*A beat.*

A toast.

**SIMON** *encourages* **RUMI** *to clink their empty glasses.* **RUMI** *is still staring at the floor where he poured the drink.*

*Lights down.*

## Scene Five

*Lights rise on* **SIMON** *and* **RUMI** *at the mosque, helping to set up for the Eid party. They arrange plastic cutlery and plates.*

**SIMON**  Food smells amazing. Cannot wait.

**RUMI**  ...

**SIMON**  It's from that place I was telling you about, that I saw on my way home the other day. Their chicken biryani is spot on.

**RUMI**  Yeah?

**SIMON**  I mean, not as good as your mum's. That's just... *(beat)* You alright?

**RUMI**  Not feeling too great. I might go.

**SIMON**  It's my first proper Eid.

**RUMI**  Sorry.

*A pause.*

**SIMON**  I know I've been harsh on you.

**RUMI**  ...

**SIMON**  You grew up with all this stuff.

**RUMI**  I did.

**SIMON**  Shouldn't be difficult for you to fall back into it.

**RUMI**  Theoretically...

*Beat.*

**SIMON**  But if your heart's not in it—

**RUMI**  Then what? What are you going to do? Go back?

**SIMON**  I can't undiscover everything.

**RUMI**  ...

**SIMON** I've opened my heart to God, people have taken me in, accepted me as this new person and I can't let them down. Can't let myself down. Don't want to let you down.

*Silence.*

**RUMI** I think I'm going to go.

**SIMON** Don't, not now. It's just before dinner.

**RUMI** I really don't feel well.

**SIMON** What will everyone say?

**RUMI** Who the fuck cares?

**SIMON** Rumi!

**RUMI** Just tell them it's a migraine, insinuate I'm pregnant.

**SIMON** Are you?

**RUMI** Oh you'd love that. Think of the brownie points. Your virile Muslamic seed fertilising my dingy atheist womb. Barren and forlorn, it was uninhabitable until you came along.

**SIMON** Rumi—

**RUMI** Stay. It's your first Eid, you deserve to enjoy it.

**SIMON** I can't if you leave.

**RUMI** Sorry.

> **RUMI** *rushes out. As she is exiting,* **IRFAN** *enters, blocking her path.*

**IRFAN** Eid Mubarak, Rumi. Thank you for volunteering your time. And allowing Simon to spend so much time with us recently, we have enjoyed his company.

**RUMI** You're welcome. Excuse me.

*He goes to ask her if she's okay, but she's too fast.*

**IRFAN** Brother Saeed! Eid Mubarak.

**SIMON** Eid Mubarak, Irfan.

*The two embrace.*

**IRFAN**  Rumi okay?

**SIMON**  Not really.

**IRFAN**  I'm sorry to hear—

**SIMON**  I need to talk to you, get your opinion.

**IRFAN**  It is Eid day, Simon—

**SIMON**  I feel like she's mocking me constantly. She's not interested in learning—

**IRFAN**  We should really talk about this another time, when there's less—

**SIMON**  Can you tell her please?

**IRFAN**  Simon, you can't persuade—

**SIMON**  I'm trying to be a good man, a good person. But she insists on being defiant, and...it feels like I'm dragging her along. Kicking and screaming.

**IRFAN**  You have to be tolerant of each other. Talk to each other, find a way to—

**SIMON**  I've put in so much time and effort in my learning and—

**IRFAN**  A marriage needs work, Simon. It's not easy.

**SIMON**  And I just want to pick her up and put her on the right path. Like you said, you said I have to guide her, remember?

**IRFAN**  That's why I recommended you come see me together.

**SIMON**  I'm reading scriptures to try and find advice but... Show me a passage of the text / I can use to show her...

**IRFAN**  / Simon, you can't use the Quran to control your wife. That is not how it works.

**SIMON**  So what?

**IRFAN** You came to me with an open heart. Now you must allow
   Rumi to explore what is in hers. Love of God is love of wife.
   Take care of her. That's your only job. Do you understand?

**SIMON** Yes. I think I have to go.

**IRFAN** Go.

   **SIMON** *rushes out after* **RUMI.** *Lights fade on* **IRFAN.**

## Scene Six

*Lights rise on* **RUMI**, *staring at the stars in the same spot her and* **SIMON** *were at over a year ago.* **SIMON** *runs onstage. When* **RUMI** *doesn't react, he approaches her. They both watch the stars in silence for a moment.*

**RUMI**  Have you ever seen a nebula?

**SIMON**  No.

**RUMI**  Looks like candy floss.

**SIMON**  ...

**RUMI**  Saw it through a telescope. Just about. Pinkey and purple. I think. I don't know. I can't actually remember whether there was colour, or if I'm superimposing a memory of a picture in an encyclopaedia onto a memory of a telescope. Weird how the brain does that. *(beat)* All I know is that I saw a nebula once, through a telescope. It was dark, couldn't have been London, must have been...

**SIMON**  ...

**RUMI**  Is it late? I should have told you I was here.

**SIMON**  It's okay.

**RUMI**  Is it?

**SIMON**  Yes.

*A pause.*

**RUMI**  Do you remember the first time we came here? And you freaked out because I suggested you'd have to convert.

**SIMON**  ...

**RUMI**  I was trying to push you away. Didn't think you'd actually want to do it.

*A pause.*

**SIMON** Thank you for my present.

**RUMI** So you've been home?

**SIMON** An Eid tree is just the kind of tradition I'd like to start with you. Rumi, it was beautiful, so much nicer than any Christmas tree I ever had.

*A pause.*

**RUMI** How was the rest of the party?

**SIMON** Fine.

**RUMI** No one said anything?

**SIMON** No one noticed.

**RUMI** Not even Irfan?

*A pause.*

**SIMON** What's alternative Rumi doing right now?

**RUMI** Staring at us, staring at them.

**SIMON** Celebrating...what's the opposite of Eid?

**RUMI** What does it feel like...that thing you're feeling?

**SIMON** What do you mean?

**RUMI** Certainty? Safety? Security? How does it feel to be so sure—

**SIMON** Did you mean it when you called yourself an atheist?

**RUMI** Do you think people can tell just by looking at me? Do you think they all know I'm a fraud?

**SIMON** You're not a fraud.

**RUMI** Aren't I? I've spent my life lying about who I am and what I believe in. Sometimes I wonder if I've told so many lies they've all come true, or I've got so tangled and sucked in to them that really this *is* who I am, some sort of half person with one foot in one world and the other in another, trying to be a part of both, but in reality not even existing.

*A pause.*

**SIMON**  I didn't know.

**RUMI**  *I* didn't know. *(beat)* That's a lie. Always knew I'd never... I thought we'd—

**SIMON**  Let me help you find peace.

**RUMI**  How?

**SIMON**  Irfan says—

**RUMI**  Irfan, Irfan, Irfan. Who is Irfan to you? To us?

**SIMON**  Okay, no Irfan. Just me and you, at the mosque. We'll read books, we'll pray. There's a part of you that has faith, I know it. You're a good person, I just need you to believe it.

**RUMI**  How can I believe it when you don't.

**SIMON**  What makes you say that?

**RUMI**  Everything that's come out of your mouth recently.

**SIMON**  I admit our lives have changed slightly.

**RUMI**  Slightly.

**SIMON**  I don't regret anything. For the first time I feel I have purpose.

*Pause.*

**RUMI**  How does that make you feel?

**SIMON**  Scared. Determined. I know that this is something I want to explore. You can't tell me that just because it's not for you it can't be for me too.

**RUMI**  I know.

**SIMON**  We're a team.

**RUMI**  We are.

**SIMON**  Let me make you happy.

*SIMON reaches for* **RUMI***'s hand. She lets him take it.*

*Lights fade.*

**End of Act Two**

# ACT THREE

## Scene One

*Lights rise on* **RUMI** *and* **SIMON**'s *flat.* **IRFAN** *and* **RUMI** *are on the sofa drinking tea. After a moment* **SIMON** *enters the flat and listens to their conversation.*

**RUMI** I make excellent pakoras.

**IRFAN** So it's sorted. You will make the pakoras and I'll have one of the other women arrange tea.

**RUMI** I can do that too.

**IRFAN** Are you sure?

**RUMI** Of course, we have an urn somewhere.

**IRFAN** I must say, Rumi, it's wonderful to have you on board.

**RUMI** It's a great cause.

**IRFAN** And you're sure Simon can take care of the flyers? We'll reimburse you—

**RUMI** Not a problem. He can do it at work.

**IRFAN** Dream team, you two.

**RUMI** Whatever little we can do.

**IRFAN** May Allah shower his blessings on you.

**SIMON** *enters the room.*

**SIMON** What are you signing me up for?

**RUMI** Community day. You're cool with that, aren't you?

**SIMON** I heard something about pakoras.

IRFAN You raved about how good Rumi's are, so I asked her if she wouldn't mind sharing.

SIMON Aw, babe, that's great.

RUMI Are you going to help me cook them, Simon?

SIMON I agreed to drive a couple of the lads to the hospital to see some elders. It's flu season.

IRFAN I can't thank you enough for all your help this month. It's been invaluable. Both of you.

RUMI You're welcome.

IRFAN The young ones especially enjoyed your story time, Rumi, we'd love to make that a regular thing.

SIMON If you need anything else for next weekend let us know.

IRFAN I will.

IRFAN *stands.*

I'll see myself out. You both enjoy your evening.

SIMON As-salamu alaykum.

RUMI Bye.

IRFAN *exits.*

SIMON *embraces* RUMI *and they kiss.*

SIMON Missed you today. Sounds like you've been busy.

RUMI Have.

SIMON Big news. I submitted the grant application. If it's successful, we'll have a full-time soup kitchen and part-time night shelter. Inshallah.

RUMI Fingers crossed.

SIMON Let's celebrate.

RUMI Saturday. There's that new steak house.

**SIMON**  Yes! Perfect, it's halal too.

**RUMI**  Yup.

**SIMON**  The guys'll love that.

**RUMI**  Guys?

**SIMON**  Everyone at the event.

**RUMI**  ...

**SIMON**  No?

**RUMI**  I was thinking we could do just us.

**SIMON**  Well, that looks rude when we're all in one place and then we leave. No?

**RUMI**  I guess.

**SIMON**  Hold on. I got you something. Close your eyes.

*He takes a present out from under the sofa.*

Go on. Open it.

**RUMI** *does. Carefully. It is a scarf.*

The women are wearing it kind of like a turban, but I think you could wear it more traditionally as well. The colours will really suit you.

**RUMI**  It's pretty. And soft.

**SIMON**  Do you like it?

**RUMI**  It's very kind of you—

**SIMON**  Do you want help? I watched a YouTube video.

**RUMI**  Of course you did.

**SIMON**  You don't like it.

**RUMI**  It's a very pretty scarf. Thank you.

**SIMON**  I love you.

**RUMI**  I love you.

**SIMON** *grabs* **RUMI** *for a kiss and then exits.*

*After a moment,* **RUMI** *retreats to her world. It's been a while since she's been there. She waits for* **RIZ.** *When there's nothing for a moment, she calls out.*

Divorce is worse than marrying him in the first place.

*She waits for a response. Nothing. She starts to tie the hijab slowly, morosely.*

You're awfully quiet.

*She waits for a response. Nothing.*

You know it is.

*She waits for a response. Nothing.*

I'll take your silence as agreement then. Right. Let's do this, Rumi. Let's do this.

*Lights fade.*

## Scene Two

*Lights rise on the streets outside the mosque where* **SIMON**
*is handing out flyers and cups of tea. He wears a thobe*
*and a plain white kufi hat. He is sometimes heckled.*
*All heckler voices are presented as a voiceover.*

**SIMON**  Free tea! Join us to raise money for the homeless.

**HECKLER**  Fuck off, just trying to convert people. You lot are all the same.

**SIMON**  Mate. It's charity. Cup of tea and a chat with someone that really needs it.

**HECKLER**  You're all a bunch of kiddy-fiddlers.

**SIMON**  …

**HECKLER**  You're a shame to white people.

**SIMON**  Have a pakora, they're really good.

**HECKLER**  You just want to be a terrorist towel-head, mate.

**SIMON**  Why don't you come over here and say that to my face.

**HECKLER**  Bring back British culture!

**SIMON**  I'm English.

**HECKLER**  Nah mate, you're a fucking traitor, giving out flyers with Allah Allah Sharia Law on it.

**SIMON**  You don't have to take one.

**HECKLER**  Get out! And take all those foreign scroungers with you.

**SIMON**  You know there are five times as many UK citizens receiving social welfare in Ireland?

**HECKLER**  Go fuck a goat.

**SIMON**  Thanks for the advice, you—

*SIMON sees RUMI approaching and immediately disengages with the argument. RUMI is dressed in an abaya with her head covered. She sees SIMON and walks over. They have a quick, awkward kiss.*

Asalamualaikum.

**RUMI** I've brought more rations. They're inside.

*RUMI hands a thermos to SIMON.*

And for you, masala tea.

**SIMON** Aw thanks, babe, that's really nice.

**RUMI** What's the reception been like?

**SIMON** It's been good. People have been nice, signing up for the soup kitchen. We've had a couple of EDL types, but nothing serious.

**RUMI** You're not attracting negative attention?

**SIMON** Nothing I can't handle.

*From offstage someone is calling for Brother Saeed.*

Just a minute, brother.

**RUMI** What – what did he just call you?

**SIMON** The ladies are just over there. Why don't you—

**RUMI** Simon...?

**SIMON** Yes, babe?

**RUMI** Did he just call you Saeed? Have you changed your name?

**SIMON** It started as, you know, poking fun, but I kind of like it.

**RUMI** Saeed?

**SIMON** Did you bring biscuits too?

**RUMI** What else haven't you told me?

**SIMON** You look beautiful, Rumi.

RUMI  Am I supposed to call you Saeed now?

SIMON  Husband is just fine.

RUMI  ...

SIMON  It's not a big thing, babe—

RUMI  If you're changing your name, I'd argue it is.

SIMON  It – it's nothing. Just a joke, a connection between us – the men – people like calling me Saeed. It's a cool name.

RUMI  Real cool. *(beat)* Saeed.

SIMON  You don't like it?

RUMI  No. It's not—

SIMON  What's the problem?

RUMI  Oh nothing. Just that this is the first I hear about it. I'm your wife and you don't even tell me you've changed your name. Some guy is calling you Saeed—

SIMON  We talked about this way back, when I first—

RUMI  What else are you not telling me? What else are you hiding?

SIMON  It's not a big deal Rumi, I'm not hiding anything. We can talk about this later on. It's just some guy calling—

RUMI  Calling you Saeed, yeah, I heard.

SIMON  Don't. Don't... It's just a name.

RUMI  It's not just a name.

SIMON  Why don't you go join the women?

RUMI  What?

SIMON  The women are over there, why don't you go—

RUMI  I'm okay. Fine right here. Next to my husband Saeed.

SIMON  Please don't do this now.

RUMI  I'm not doing anything. I'm literally just standing here.

SIMON  People expect me... You should. Can you just go sit with the women.

RUMI  Nah, I'm alright.

SIMON  Go sit with the women. Please.

RUMI  I helped organise this whole thing.

SIMON  I'm in the middle of something.

RUMI  No bother. I can stand by you, Saeed, as you do your important work.

SIMON  It *is* important.

RUMI  I can tell, you're getting all agitated.

SIMON  I am not getting... Why are you defying me?

RUMI  I am sure you can help God's people with your humble wife next to you. I'm sure the mullahs won't forbid you from that? Or does the Quran say that women can't do God's work? I can't remember. You know though? Don't you? You're the expert—

SIMON  You're being disrespectful.

RUMI  To who?

SIMON  Please don't show me up like this, not in front of everyone.

RUMI  Am I embarrassing you? Are you ashamed of me? Your heathen wife.

SIMON  Right now, I am. I am ashamed of you.

RUMI  Oh really, well...

*She begins to uncover her head and take off her abaya.*

SIMON  Don't you dare. Put that back on.

RUMI  Remember the first time you saw me like this, Saeed? Or does that not count because it was Simon?

SIMON  Rumi, don't. Put that back on. PUT THAT BACK ON!

RUMI  Or what? What are you going to do, Saeed?

SIMON  Please. Please put that on, Rumi, don't do this. Not here.

RUMI  What are you going to do if I don't? What, Saeed? What are you going to do?

SIMON  Rumi.

*She continues to take off her abaya and layers.* SIMON *picks up the headscarf and tries to wrap it around her head. They struggle.* SIMON *hits* RUMI. *They freeze. He goes to touch her face where his blow landed.*

RUMI  *(shouting)* DON'T YOU FUCKING DARE. DON'T YOU DARE TELL ME WHAT TO DO, HOW TO LIVE MY LIFE. YOU'RE A JOKE. YOU KNOW FUCK ALL AND YOU'RE HERE BECAUSE YOU... WHY ARE YOU HERE? LOOK AT THEM, LAUGHING AT YOU. YOU THINK THEY TAKE YOU SERIOUSLY? YOU'RE MAKING A MOCKERY OF THE RELIGION AND A FOOL OF YOURSELF. YOU'RE A FUCKING JOKE.

*She exits, leaving* SIMON *standing holding her hijab.*

*Lights down.*

## Scene Three

RUMI *is asleep on the sofa. She was up all night waiting for* SIMON, *who didn't come home. As lights rise,* RUMI *stirs. After a moment she awakes with a start, checks the time and picks up her phone to call* SIMON *again. The doorbell rings.* RUMI *goes to answer the door and is surprised to see* IRFAN.

IRFAN  As-salamu alaykum, Rumi.

RUMI  Salaam.

IRFAN  How are you doing?

RUMI  I'm okay. *(Beat.)* Simon's not here, so...

IRFAN  Something happened and...I think it's best if we... Can I sit down?

RUMI *reluctantly lets* IRFAN *in. They sit.*

IRFAN  Yesterday. After you left. There was an...altercation. He was provoked and...he was arrested. They kept him overnight, at the police station. He called me this morning and—

RUMI  He called you?

IRFAN  Yes. And I thought the first person—

RUMI  He called you from the police station?

IRFAN  So I came here as soon as... Rumi, I know things have been difficult between you two, that you've experienced some difficulties—

RUMI  Were those his words? Difficulties?

IRFAN  Simon—

RUMI  Back to calling him Simon, are we?

IRFAN  I'm not taking sides, Rumi, and please, let me say that you are definitely not at fault here.

RUMI  Damn straight I'm not.

IRFAN  Our job now is to help—

RUMI  Our job? My husband is in police custody and instead of calling me, he calls you!

IRFAN  He's feeling vulnerable.

RUMI  He hit me! Yesterday, in front of everyone. But of course we wouldn't want *him* to feel any more vulnerable or unsafe. So why don't you tell him, from me, that it's best if we just leave this.

*This is news to* IRFAN, *he tries to find the right response.*

IRFAN  You've been treated unfairly, Rumi, I see that, I didn't know—

RUMI  Please could you tell Simon, I assume that as his spiritual advisor you'll be seeing him?

IRFAN  I will.

RUMI  He's not welcome here.

IRFAN  I beg you to reconsider.

RUMI  Thank you for coming, and for delivering the message.

RUMI *gets up and ushers* IRFAN *to the door.*

IRFAN  Rumi, don't throw this away. I can mediate. Simon needs you, he's hurting and lost—

RUMI  I can't.

IRFAN  Help him find that man that first came to me with so much enthusiasm—

RUMI  No.

IRFAN  So much love for you—

Please.

RUMI *shuts the door in his face and collapses onto the floor. After a moment she goes to open the door and call* IRFAN *back, but stops. She sits, lamenting, until jumping up and starting to pack. She grabs things that aren't even very helpful, but anything to fill the bag, a woman on a mission. Then, stillness as she takes in the gravity of what's happened.*

RIZ *speaks, as if from nowhere.*

RIZ  Motherfucking, shit-bricking asshole. Penchod! [**asshole in Punjabi**]

RUMI  You can't talk about an imaam like that.

RIZ  Meant Simon.

RUMI  Him either. Don't.

RIZ  Why? We're leaving.

RUMI  Am I?

RIZ  Yes.

*A long pause.* RUMI *comes to term, with the fact that she's leaving.*

RUMI  I'm leaving. *(beat)* I am—

RIZ  Fierce.

RUMI  And—

RIZ  Determined.

RUMI  And—

RIZ  And dheet [**stubborn**] and insensitive and—

RUMI  Just fine being me.

RIZ  Finally.

*A beat.*

Enjoy the freedom. Live as much as possible. And for fucks sake, no more white boys.

**RUMI**  No more boys full stop.

**RIZ**  Give it time, be chasing peen soon enough.

**RUMI**  No way.

**RIZ**  Way.

*Lights fade as* **RUMI** *continues to pack.*

## Scene Four

*Two years later and* **RUMI** *and* **SIMON** *are divorced.*
*They haven't spoken but* **RUMI** *knows* **SIMON** *is still*
*practising Islam. He knows she is still single. Lights*
*snap up on* **RUMI** *centre stage at her stand-up show.*
*She speaks into a microphone, confident and sassy. The*
*audience love her.*

**RUMI** This one guy Facebook – stalked me when I was in the
bathroom. Short attention span was red-flag number 1.

Red-flag number 2 – upon my return he said...

*(full on Essex accent)* Wow, you're like super-efnic, right?

I almost spat my Rioja at him in surprise.

He'd obviously seen the profile picture of me dressed as a
Christmas bauble at my cousin's very Pakistani wedding last
year and assumed that was how I spent the majority of my
waking life. So I gave up white boys and went halal speed
dating. And it was just as you can imagine.

*Beat.*

Fucking awful. There I was, thinking I'd walk into a room of
modern Muslim men from a variety of cultural backgrounds
and we'd bond over our shared experiences of growing up
in east London and sneaking out of our parents' houses.
Instead I got passport boy. Why is he called passport boy?
Because all he said was—

**RUMI** *plays* **PASSPORT BOY** *with a very Indian accent.*

**PASSPORT BOY** You British? Have passport? I lowe you. [**love**]

**RUMI** Then, then we have Ahmed, who I must say was rather
handsome. And Ahmed says—

**RUMI** *plays* **AHMED** *with a thick Middle Eastern accent.*

**AHMED** Sister. What is your job?

RUMI  Apparently calling women sister is an Arab thing and not weird at all.

AHMED  Sister. You are easily distracted, we only have three minutes.

RUMI  Alright.

AHMED  What is your job?

RUMI  Well I—

AHMED  Tick tock.

RUMI  My day job is admin, boring stuff, but I'm also a food blogger.

AHMED  I see. And what do you like to eat?

RUMI  I enjoy all the fine dining restaurants London has to offer.

AHMED  Tell me your favourite.

RUMI  Le Gavroche.

AHMED  French?

RUMI  Mais oui.

AHMED  And what you eat there?

RUMI  Coquilles St Jacques Grillées et boudin noir.

AHMED  This is?

RUMI  Grilled Scallops and black pudding.

AHMED  Delicious. But what is this black pudding?

*A beat.*

RUMI  And so I told him. Then we just sat there staring at each other until the bell rang.

Oh. I left out a crucial detail. I did all this dressed in a full abaya and hijab, proper ninja style. Why you ask? Pfft. Because I thought pretending to look like a devout Muslim would be the best way to attract a dude that's looking for a non-practising, booze guzzling, do whatever the fuck she likes, kinda gal.

*Beat.*

I guess I wasn't ready to be honest with myself, to appreciate just how fine I am being this version of me. A really fit Pakistani guy once called me a coconut. When I told him I didn't like it, he said it was probably because I was one. Well, guess what mister? That was then. Now, *now* you can call me whatever name you want, but I'm happy just being Rumi.

Thank you all, you've been wonderful. I hope you have a great night.

*Rapturous applause.* **RUMI** *takes a bow. As she rises she spots* **SIMON** *at the back of the room and waves. She makes her way over to him.*

Hi.

**SIMON**  That was something else.

**RUMI**  Thank you. Thanks, I – I didn't know you—

**SIMON**  I saw you in *Timeout*. One to watch.

**RUMI**  Apparently.

**SIMON**  How are you? You look great.

**RUMI**  Good. I mean, I'm here! It's still... *(beat)* You look well.

**SIMON**  I feel well. You look... You were amazing up there. So confident. How have you been?

**RUMI**  Good. Doing well.

**SIMON**  You're happy?

**RUMI**  Yeah.

**SIMON**  Good.

**RUMI**  And you?

**SIMON**  I – I'm. I'm really good.

RUMI ...

SIMON My Arabic's coming along and I...I've been helping out at the night shelter, actually I'm managing that. So—

RUMI That's great. That's big—

SIMON What have you been up to?

RUMI This. Um, this is going surprisingly well...

SIMON I'm not surprised! You're hilarious.

RUMI What else? Are you...

SIMON Not much, just... Work. Was that the night we met? After the speed dating?

RUMI Yeah—

SIMON Oh. *(beat)* Next time you should tell the one about the white guy that walks into a mosque.

RUMI ...

SIMON Is this weird? I knew you'd be here and I just wanted to—

RUMI No...it was good to see you.

SIMON It is so good to see you. Yeah. And I – I guess I'll see you around. On the telly?!

RUMI Maybe.

*He goes to walk away.*

Simon.

SIMON Yeah?

RUMI I'm sorry.

SIMON Me too.

*Lights down.*

**End of Play**

# THIS IS NOT THE END